LOVING THE IMPERFECT MAN

CHARA A. TAYLOR

LOVE CLONES
publishing

Love Clones Publishing
www.lcpublishing.net

Printed in the **United States** of America

First Printing, 2015

ISBN: 978-0692517581

King James Version Scripture quotations marked "KJV" are taken from the Holy Bible, King James Version (Public Domain).

New King James Version
Scripture quotations marked "NKJV" are taken from the New King James Version. Copyright © 1982 by Thomas Nelson, Inc. Used by permission. All rights reserved.

Publishers:
Love Clones Publishing
Dallas, TX 75205
www.lcpublishing.net

Dedication

This book is dedicated to my wonderful and loving husband: Bishop Ronald E. Taylor Jr. Being married to you has been a constant gift that presents me with wonderful surprises daily. Your pure heart makes it easy to love and respect you! I love you! You are so breathtaking. I love the way you love me.

I would also like to dedicate this book to every wife that desires to be the wife that Ephesians 5 talks about – you can do it! Trust God, follow His guidelines, embrace your marriage, and enjoy the benefits!

Special Thanks

Giving glory to God - the author and the orchestrator of my existence! Thank You Lord for creating me, equipping me, strengthening me, purifying me, and qualifying me for Your awesome institution of marriage. Thank You Lord for allowing me to share with the world what You have taught me about covenant and unyielding love. My love for You is modeled in how I treat the man of God and I thank You for not giving up on me!

Acknowledgements

I want to say THANK YOU to my husband, Bishop Ronald Taylor Jr., for allowing me to write this transparent book which will share our moments – good and bad - with the world. Thanks for trusting God's plan for our marriage – many marriages will be saved through our testimony. Thank you for always funding my different projects! I love you!

I want to thank the godly Kingdom couples who live and lead as examples and who have poured into us individually and as a couple: Pastors Willie and Cecilia Holloway of Gospel Power Christian Church of St. Louis, Missouri and Apostles Robbie and Sharon Peters of The Empowerment Word and Truth Church of Chicago, IL.

I want to thank all the ministry wives in my life who sense me in the spirit, pray with me, and hold me accountable to being a godly wife: Apostle Alois M. Bell, Apostle Tonya Stewart, Prophetess Alicia Mosley, Apostle Sharon Peters, and Minister Anise Braggs. I love you all and I appreciate the times you have been there for prayer and encouragement. You never judged Bishop or me; you've never spoken a negative word about him. I appreciate all of you dearly and I could not have made this journey without your support and godly guidance. You are genuine women of faith and true kingdom wives! Thank you for all you have imparted into my life!

To my apostolic dad, Apostle Robbie C. Peters, thank you for being more than a great leader; you have given me words of wisdom and encouragement I needed from a father's perspective. You never judged me and always provided support. I have grown immensely as a wife since you came into our lives. You have helped me to see what a man really needs from his wife. I appreciate your gentle rebukes and soft corrections to help me be the wife I'm called to be. The Robbie and Sharon Virtuous Principles (RSVP) BlogTalk Radio show, with you and Mom (Apostle Sharon Peters), is the real deal when it comes to giving couples what is needed to live holy and happy as married couples in ministry.

I would like to thank my Sisters (Deborah, Tavera, & Ann Cheree) and my Mother (Betty Bevley) for being a loving family. You love my husband and I appreciate it! You treat him like he is your very own. Thanks for always being there for him and making him feel accepted! You are a great family and I love you! A special thank you to our godfather, Deacon Jimmy Wilder, who saw God's vision and plan for us as a kingdom couple from the very beginning. You have always encouraged us and have been a great friend for Bishop. I appreciate you!

Finally, I want to say, "God bless you," to an awesome publisher: Candace N. Ford of Love Clones Publishing for making this book happen. Thank you for your talented professional work. I appreciate you!

Table of Contents

Foreword

Everybody wants LOVE, but unfortunately it is so misunderstood, even by many who are believers! How can this be when I John 4:8 tells us that GOD IS LOVE, yet God fearing believers still misinterpret love every day in their relationships? The man/woman relationship suffers and is suffering greatly while the divorce rate continues to increase because even marital love is miscommunicated in our relationships as husband and wife!

However, God used love and kindness to draw us! The Bible lets us know in Romans 5:8 that while we were yet sinners or in such an imperfect state of being, God extended his love towards us by sending His Son Jesus Christ to die on the cross for us! Therefore, in these last evil days, we as people of God must do a better job of communicating love to an imperfect world! If you wait for a person to become excellent in their ways in order to extend love to them, don't bother because you have just miscommunicated the very essence of the God-kind of love!

In this book, the author takes us on a "love walk" as she allows us to review her personal failures and successes as one who had to learn to love like God through her own holy experience with Christ our Savior! She shows us that love (when it is perfected) will cast out all fear! She demonstrates to us, through this book, how love heals and mends that which is broken in a relationship!

As you read this book, you will be loosed to love and you will be even more equipped to love like God! Not only will this book show you the importance in loving the imperfections of a man, it will also cause you to see the beauty of "marital covenant" which should cause you to strive even more in letting love bring forth the fullness of God in your Covenant Union!

Dr. Sharon R. Peters

A Loving Wife to Dr. Robbie C. Peters of
The Empowerment Word & Truth Church

Introduction

Marriage is not meant to make you happy; marriage is meant to make you holy! Couples do experience the spiritual element of joy in marriage and along the way there are happy and fun times; but to think that marriage will make you "happy" is a false perception of why our Creator designed this incredible covenant. Marriage is designed to help you fulfill your purpose, not to make you prosperous. Prosperity is one of the many benefits we get to enjoy in the marriage. The truth is that a person can have prosperity and times of "happiness" and joy without being married; therefore, the mission of marriage should not be for happiness or financial gain. Marriage is meant to make you holy because marriage is ministry. In marriage we will find ourselves on the Potter's wheel being shaped, molded, and refined in areas that are not fruitful in our life. If we allow marriage to perfect (mature) us: we will grow out of selfishness, learn how to love unconditionally, understand the fullness of forgiveness, learn effective communication and letting your words be seasoned with grace, walk in reverence, submission, and respect, and understand the power of unity. You will increase in areas of intercession and prayer, trusting God, and meekness. You will receive deliverance in areas of rejection, anger, bitterness, control, manipulation, fear, and pride. You will grow from being independent to being interdependent. Again, marriage is not meant to make you happy, it's meant to make you holy. These attributes of the Godhead and more will manifest in our lives and marriage if we follow God's divine layout for marriage, and reject what we saw while growing up in our homes, reject what we have heard from nonbelievers or unsaved individuals, reject the worldly view of marriage, and even reject the world's opportunity to escape from marriage. Your marriage does not have to resemble the generations of marital problems from your blood line; your marriage can resemble the beauty of oneness it was created to illustrate.

I was not one of the women who desired marriage. I had not asked the Lord for a husband; and honestly I did not see myself as "wife material"- whatever that means. I convinced myself that all I wanted to do was serve God and do His will for my life. I did not realize that I was attempting to escape hurt and pain; I was protecting myself by wanting to stay to myself; I was dodging being shaped and refined. All along, a part of God's will for my life was to be married to the man of God He had purposed for me. The same is true for you! Just because the man God has ordained for you to marry is a man of God does not mean the marriage journey will be easy. Marriage is formed of two very imperfect people coming together in oneness to make a unified, harmonious, God-led impact in the earth realm that will cause God to be glorified, cause others to be unified, and cause Kingdom growth in earthly vessels. Godly marriage will in no way resemble what the world considers marriage. A godly marriage will draw and not separate. A godly marriage will be attacked and suffer afflictions, but the Lord will deliver them from every affliction. A godly marriage is beautiful - filled with the splendor and glory of God. A godly marriage raises children in the admonition of the Lord. A godly marriage seeks to live according to Holy Scripture. The only way to have a godly marriage is to practice biblical standards and instructions for marriage. Each gender is flawed and should be loved in spite of their imperfections, just as God loves us regardless of our imperfections. This book will examine what the godly marriage looks like and give practical tips to assist your growth in a godly marriage through divine revelations and prophetic wisdom in how to love the man in his imperfection.

CHAPTER 1

THE INSTITUTION OF MARRIAGE

The Merriam Webster dictionary defines marriage as "the relationship that exists between a husband and a wife" and "the state of being united to a person of the opposite sex as husband or wife in a consensual and contractual recognized law" (web 1). This is a fair and accurate description of what marriage is designed to be from a natural and carnal perspective. Due to the fact that we are called to live in this world but not of this world, we need more than the carnal perspective of what marriage is designed to look like. It is imperative to see marriage the way God sees marriage and live according to the layout He gave us in His Holy Word. In Genesis, He gives us a solid picture of what He had in mind when He created the institution of marriage. From the scripture Genesis 2:18, 21-24, we have the very first wedding, from which we can conclude that God's idea for marriage was designed and instituted by the Creator Himself and that His heart and design for marriage is companionship and intimacy between a natural born male and natural born female. Let us look at what the scripture says.

"And the LORD God said, "It is not good that man should be alone; I will make him a helper comparable to him" (Genesis 2:18)

"And the LORD God caused a deep sleep to fall on Adam and he slept; and He (God) took one of his ribs and closed up the flesh in its place. Then the rib which the LORD God had taken from man He (God) made (built) into a woman and He (God) brought her to the

man. And Adam said, 'This is now bone of my bones and flesh of my flesh. She shall be called 'Woman' because she was taken out of 'Man.''' Therefore a man shall leave his father and mother and be joined to his wife and they shall become one flesh"

(Genesis 2:21-24)

The beginning of verse 28, God says, *"It is not good for man to be alone."* Immediately God recognized the man He created was in an imperfect situation! This imperfection was not overlooked and God could have easily just made the man perfect in his aloneness. Yet, God decided that the man didn't need to be left alone, the man needed a helper. God does not expect the man to be perfect in the sense of being blameless and without mistakes; God expects man to do his best, follow His commands, and live according to the plan He has laid out for his life. Further, in verse 18 of Genesis 2, the LORD God said that He would make Adam a helper comparable to him. For Adam to have a "helper" indicates that Adams strength for all he was called to do was inadequate in itself. This is not saying that Adam was incapable of fulfilling what he was called to do but that he could use a little assistance. His helper is made comparable to him, which actually means complimentary. She was made to complement him not compete with him. The complementary helper was created to meet the needed help for daily work, procreation, and mutual support through companionship. She was not created to compete with him for titles, position, leadership, gifts, anointing, parenting, intellect, cooking ability, physique, financial dominance or anything else. No, we were put together to complement one another and to have our gifts gel together to impact the Kingdom.

One of my husband's dominate gifts is gift of

knowledge and one of my primary gifts is gift of wisdom. In the beginning of the marriage we didn't know how to work together so our gifts gelled; therefore, we were a mess. We found ourselves competing, out talking one another, not trusting one another's gifts, it was terrible. Individually we were fine, but he needed the wisdom that God has given me to help him with knowing when to use his knowledge. On the other hand, I needed his knowledge because I was excellent at application and not content and context. Once we learned that God wanted us to gel together we began to see instant manifestations of prosperity in all areas of our life. Ask yourself what your individual gifts are and how do they work hand in hand? Make a commitment to use your gifts to glorify God by becoming one with your husband.

In verses 21-24, God puts Adam in a deep sleep, took one of his ribs, and closed Adams flesh. God then takes the rib from Adam and uses it to build the woman. After God built the woman, then God brought her to the man. Upon seeing the woman Adam said, *"This is now bone of my bones and flesh of my flesh, she shall be called Woman because she was taken out of Man."* It is this reason that a man shall leave his father and mother and be joined (cleave) to his wife and they shall become one flesh. In these few verses of scripture, we see several principles that shape marriage. The first one is found in verse 21. God put Adam to sleep, removed his rib, and closed his flesh. Wives, this tells us that only God can change the man. The man will not change by our negative words, sassy attitudes, ongoing nagging, and definitely not our gymnastic skills in the bed. The change we desire to see will only manifest under God's scalpel. God has to perform surgery on the man and He has to put him back together (or heal him). I implore you, Woman of God, to stop attempting to change the man. The fact is that if you could have changed him then you would have changed him by now; but changing him is not part of the job description of the wife. Complementing him does not include changing him, it means enhancing him. Ketchup does not change a hamburger, it enhances the taste of the burger. Same is with the wife, we don't change the man, our help enhances him in every area of his life. The next important truth to consider from this passage is in verse 22. God took the rib from Adam and He (God) built the woman. Too many times we find ourselves looking to be built by our husband or people in general. Or even worse, we decide we are going to build ourselves by copying what we see in the world. Here in scripture, we see that the building of woman is not in the husband's job description – it can only accurately and effectively be done by God. At a recent women's conference I attended, Apostle Sharon Peters said, "If man builds us then we are built to perform, but if we allow God to build us then we are built to last." She went on to make us aware that if we are built to perform then we will be performing for the rest of our lives, always trying to keep up with the competition, always trying to prove ourselves. I thought about that and concluded that I am not a car - I am a woman. Cars are built to perform – they are built to run but eventually they run out of gas and need to be filled up in order to perform again. They require regular maintenance in order to perform properly and without regular upkeep they stop performing at their maximum capacity. Cars were built by man to perform. Man only has the capability of building what he likes, what he wants, what his minds perceives as functional and beautiful. This is not the will of God.

God builds excellence, man builds performance. If you want to be built to last then allow God to build you. If you want to be built by man then be prepared to be replaced when you break down. If you want to be built by man then prepare to run out of gas frequently and then hope he (man) has something to fill you back up because some men don't keep gas money and their cars are required to sit alone and untouched for long periods of time while they find a replacement. It's important to be built by God.

In this same verse, we see that God brought (or presented) her – the God built woman – to the man. And the very next verse says that Adam (upon seeing her) said, "This is now bone of my bones and flesh of my flesh, she shall be called Woman because she was taken out of Man." Here we see that immediately Adam recognized something of himself in her – immediately. Adam had been given the job of naming all the created animals; when he saw the woman he recognized her as a part of himself, then he named her. Too often we find ourselves presenting ourselves to the man. It is God's job to show or present the built woman to the man. When we present ourselves we present broken, fractured fragments of a woman seeking to be repaired by what he (the man) offers in way of appearance. When we are broken spiritually and struggling with rejection, fear, or abandonment, we can become attracted to the anointing on the man's life when we see him being used by God to edify, exhort, encourage, as he is speaking what you need to hear at that moment. The anointing on the man's life looks appealing but the truth is if you were not created for that man, you will not be equipped to handle the assignment that comes along with the anointing and you will not be equipped to handle the man because all you will ever want in operation is that anointing. When the truth is after he's done preaching and teaching you get the "man" – the fallible, fleshy man! And that side of him is not always what you see in the pulpit!

On another hand, when we've struggled financially and are bound by lack and pride, we can become attracted to material possessions and mistake it for security. This false attraction will only last until the money runs out or sickness/affliction hits. Money will be the Elmer's glue that holds you together when God should be the Super glue. This is why the wedding vows include for richer or poorer... because many only marry for money or because they were attracted to what the other person had in possession and the marriage does not last. The Scripture says that what God joins together let no man put asunder (NKJV). Marriages united by God are designed to last through the fire and test and trials, whereas, the things of man that draw couples together like money, sex, convenience, fear of loneliness, adultery, or children out of wedlock, will only last momentarily. If this is how you were joined with your spouse, I would advise seeking some spiritual counseling and getting rooted in the foundations of a scripture led marriage before what joined you together runs out. If you were joined on the things of man and you have hit the hard place of desolation with no hope of return, pray for guidance. Nothing is too hard for God to fix if it's meant to be fixed. If you are unsaved or a nonbeliever in a marriage built on money or other things of man, and you are looking to have a godly marriage, it is important for you to know that you cannot start talking to him about what scripture says and expect him to immediately change. What he sees is that you changed, he has not changed and to him you are not on the same page with him. You may be absolutely correct but it's going to take loving kindness to draw him, not words. I would encourage you to begin practicing the godly principles and spiritual disciplines within your limits and allow him to see God working and moving in your lives. Do not attempt to force him and don't go home talking about we need to tithe because that is foreign to him.

Unfortunately, others are only attracted to what the man looks like – his height, weight, skin tone, build, voice tone, etc., because low self-esteem, and perversion are lurking in your lives. These are all nice to look at but we are not to be driven by lust of any sort and the lust of the eyes always causes deception. Lust is only fulfilled temporarily, and then it's looking for its fulfillment in another person, place, or thing. Oddly enough, I must admit that as handsome as my husband is he was not "my type" physically and vice versa, I was not his type physically, yet God knew what I needed and it was not wrapped in what I perceived I wanted my husband to "look like." I know he is handsome and I am blessed to have such a handsome husband, but we were created for one another for Kingdom purposes, not to fulfill fantasy lust that came through watching movies and television shows. I would not have been open to marrying him if I had not allowed God to build me. Therefore, Woman of God, allow God to build you, heal you, deliver you, and mature you; then allow Him to present you to the man. I was presented to my husband after I was built into a woman of God who would look to God ONLY as my Source, my Provider, and my Comforter. This building up ensured that I would not idolize the man and that I would put no one before God. Being built in this area ensured that I would not put false expectations on my husband and it matured me to trust in God when times of trial, hardship, and suffering aroused in our life. Because God had built me to trust Him, times of financial difficulty brought us closer together rather than causing conflict and confusion because I was able to be the helper to him by encouraging him, lifting him up, and not nagging at him, not arguing with him, and not disrespecting him. During difficult times we seem to have the most fun together and we maintain the ability to laugh. The one time my husband lost his job and we ended up homeless for a while, it was difficult, no doubt, but being a God built woman put me in position to pray for him, and encourage him to not give up on himself. When he appeared to be sinking, and he couldn't find the strength to look for work, I stepped in and applied for jobs for him. I worked on his resume and sent it out daily. When he started getting calls for interviews, his spirits were uplifted. When he started the job, they asked him how did he hear of the position and he responded, "Honestly, I'm not sure, I think my wife must have submitted my resume to you." I never told him what I was doing, I just did it! And I bless God for the opportunity to be a vessel to help him. It's hard to see your husband down and defeated; and when the enemy has come in like a flood in his life, he needs his helper, to help him to not drown in the flood! While I was applying for jobs for him, God was giving me dreams and visions, leading me to the place we would live for the next few years and I was obedient to do everything God was leading me to do as the helper. I never overstepped my bounds and I never took the "head" role, I just merely helped him back to shallow water so he could get up and walk again. I never spoke a negative word or made him feel bad because of the situation we were in. He needed to be lifted - not left to drown.

In verse 24, we see that after the man is presented

with the woman, he recognized her as a part of himself and he named her and he was joined to her as his wife and they became one flesh. The scripture actually says, "Therefore, a man shall leave his father and mother and be joined to his wife, and they shall become one flesh" (NKJV). In this scripture, the word leave connotes a priority change on the part of the husband. This speaks of family structure for a newly married couple. It is extremely important for us to care about parents and siblings, but once married, the priority is God, spouse, children, work, extended family, and ministry. We are not to forsake our relationship with God or spouse for anything or anyone! The idea of "be joined" speaks of both passion and permanence – that is being joined passionately and permanently in all things. Finally, we see the principle of one flesh. One flesh carries several implications including sexual union, child conception, spiritual and emotional intimacy; along with showing each other the same love, attention, and respect shown to other close family members like our parents and siblings. To grasp the theological concept of unity of the couple, let us briefly look back. "In the beginning" the LORD created the couple in His image (Genesis 1:1, 27) and His description of them was "one flesh." The unity of the couple was to be so complete that the Hebrew word for 'one' – echad; or one, unit, or unity, is the same word used to describe God in Deuteronomy 6:4, "The LORD our God, the Lord is One" (NKJV). The word "God" and the word "one" are used in their plural form emphasizing the Christian doctrine of the Trinity – three Persons of the same substance in one Godhead. Just as the Father, Son, and Holy Spirit are three persons with the same substance, so it is in marriage. When man and woman are joined together they are no longer two individuals;

they have become "one being" with physical, emotional, and spiritual elements. This union is not designed to be broken or separated. Understand that because of the entrance of sin, the original unity of marriage was broken (Gen. 3:12-13) allowing strife and contention to enter the relationship (Gen 3:15), and the man and woman took on separate identities (Gen. 3:20). This was not the original design or plan when God created them in His image, but because of sin these issues are now ever present for us to contend with as couples. As believers in Jesus Christ, we are to be conformed to God's image not the image of the world. In marriage we are to reflect His image of love, unity, and marriage. We are not to reflect the world's image of marriage. Personally, I do not understand how couples have separate bank accounts, separate bills, separate household duties and responsibilities, have separate living quarters in the home, always travel separately, and yet, claim to be in unity. Once you start separating things, it becomes easy to separate ideas, plans, goals, etc. My mother used to say, "if you give the devil an inch, he will take a mile." I'm not big on clichés, but I do believe if we begin separating things we will find it easy to separate everything until we eventually separate ourselves. We will separate ourselves from one another and ultimately from God. Don't allow separation to be your reality, Trust God – be joined in all things.

CHAPTER 2

EPHESIAN 5 WIVES

"Wives submit to your own husbands as to the Lord.

For the husband is head of the wife s also Christ is the

head of the church; and He is the Savior of the body.

Therefore, just as the church is subject to Christ, so let

the wives be to their own husband in everything."

Ephesians 5:22-24 (NKJV)

These verses are loaded with dynamic marriage principles for wives to embrace. These principles, if applied and practiced, will help the wife experience joy, peace, and harmony in the marriage (in most cases). The first principle Paul presents is "submit to your own husbands as to the Lord." Oftentimes, the focal point of this verse is, *"Wives submit to your own husband,"* and yes this instruction is extremely important, but I believe if we concentrate on the second part of the verse we will find it effortless to accomplish the first. The second part is equally important. *"As unto the Lord"* stands alone as a solid foundational principal. Here is the flow of thought for the verse with the second part in its proper context; it says, "Wives submit to your own husbands as you would submit yourself to the Lord." The wife is called to submit to her husband: "as to the Lord," to respect, regard, and deeply care for him, which comes from the Greek word "phobeo "to reference" or to be in awe of" (Note 2) This points the wife toward serving her husband, honoring him, and edifying him (or building him up). Her attitude, then, according to this terminology – "as to the Lord" – is to be an attitude of highest esteem and regard for her husband, as she highly esteems and regards Jesus Christ.

Now is a great time to do some self-refection. Ask yourself, how do I submit to the Lord now and how did I submit to Him when I first gave my life to Him? More than likely, upon initial conversion to Christianity, accepting Jesus as Lord and Savior of your life, there was a level of excitement to serve Him and to know more about Him. You probably went the extra mile to please Him, attempting to live right, learn what it means to follow Him with your whole heart, etc. This is probably true even in the beginning of your marriage when you were attempting to prove to your husband that you were the one for him and you wanted him to know that you had his back. If this is the case, just keep in mind that you are not able to change up intensity of how you prove your unyielding love and support for him when the issues of life flood your path or you become overwhelmed with circumstances and situations. We are to grow and mature to a place of steadfastness being unmovable always abounding in the work of the Lord, remember your job (work) is to be a helper. You must maintain your zeal for your marriage. My apostolic mom, Apostle Sharon Peters always says, "Continue!" Continue what you have begun and if you have stopped, now is the perfect time to begin again! Here is how I started again once my eyes were opened to truth and my error. First, I repented and asked for the guidance of the Holy Spirit with my words and actions. Next, I consciously made every decision with this thought, "If it were Jesus what would I do?" I'm not saying my husband is "LORD" but my actions and words to him would be "as to the Lord." When my husband leaves for work, I ask myself "How would I treat Jesus if I knew He was leaving for work?" The answer is, if I knew Jesus was leaving for work I would encourage Him to have a wonderful productive day, I would love on Him with hugs and kisses as He leaves out the door, I would send Him with a nice warm healthy meal to nourish His body, and I would pray for Him: His safety, His mind, His productivity, His increase and war on His behalf rebuking the devour, coming against any trap set in His path, etc. Since, I would do it for Jesus, I started doing it for my husband before he leaves for work daily. I began to do this for every situation pertaining to my husband and our life. I asked myself how would I treat Jesus or prepare for Him if He was coming in from a long day of work (marketplace or ministry) and the answer is I would have a nice warm healthy meal prepared, something appropriate to drink waiting on His arrival (cold in summer, warm in the winter), house would be clean, and the atmosphere would be calm and relaxed. Yes I would do that for Jesus! If it's important enough to do it for Jesus, then it's important enough to do it for the husband. After all, husband is the head of wife.

I have the unique position of being home daily to do these things now as I'm a domestic specialist (homemaker). I did not begin the marriage as a homemaker. I did all these things while working a full time job, so I'm not just speaking from the homemaker position. I had to get creative with planning and preparation. If your marriage consists of you working outside the home and/or being a full time student, a wife, a mom, and minister, then you must get creative. The scriptures do not say this only applies to those wives who are home daily and don't work outside the house. When the Bible was written, yes, it is safe to say the women were homemakers, but due to culture change more women are outside the home working and that is fine. The culture has changed but God's word has not! Now generally the responsibilities are shared, but wife, you still have an obligation to submit to him "as to the Lord." That does not change. It doesn't matter how often the world changes, the word of God never changes. That may mean, you have to limit your social media time or your leisure time, but your obligation is home and submitting to him "as to the Lord." Yes, you have your life, but after you fulfill your duties as a wife!

The Head of Woman

"For the husband is the head of the wife as also Christ is the head of the church; and He is he Savior of the body" Ephesians 5:23 (NKJV)

This verse is not putting males over females, but it does call for husbands to accept responsible leadership in the same spirit of self-giving and devotion that Christ has shown to His church. The husband is called to lay down his life for his wife, the way Christ laid down His own life for His bride the church. The husband is to sacrifice his own interest in order to enhance the wife. The husband is called to work and provide for the wife. He is called to love the wife and make her radiant. The husband is called to keep her protected and safe. He lives the hunter-gatherer life. The husband is called to lead and rear the children, training them in the ways of the Lord. The husband's role also includes nourishment of his wife. In the Greek, nourish is "ektrpho," which is to support her growth toward her own maturity. (Strongs 1625) The husband is further called to cherish his wife. In the Greek, cherish is "thalpo," which is to warmly care for and attend to. (Strongs 2282) This lengthy list of what the husband is called to do as the head is a large responsibility. Let's also consider the weight of doing all these things in this cruel vicious world, which requires a nice home, fancy cars, 401k Plans, insurance, sufficient food, adequate clothing, and the list goes on. Yes, God is our Provider, but He is not dropping these things out of the sky and there is responsibility on our part to put our faith in action. If a man doesn't work then the man doesn't eat! The husband is working diligently to fulfill this role. The truth is, we may not agree with the work he is doing, or how he has chosen to provide. It may not make much sense to us but many of our husbands are doing their very best. You may be witnessing the error of his ways and his wrong decisions but remember he is not perfect. We may not understand why he has chosen to leave the marketplace prematurely to do full time ministry when there is not full time money coming in from his full time ministry, or his now full time ministry is taking him away from home too much. But if we keep him lifted in prayer, God definitely knows how to get his attention. Before we go any further, ask yourself,

"If he is not listening to God, why would he listen to me." Sure it's hurting you to see this, it's hurting you to see him in such inner turmoil, it's hurting you to experience this, it's hurting the relationship, it's hurting the family, it may even be hurting the ministry (if you are a wife of a husband in ministry), but consider this, it's also hurting the Lord. The Lord doesn't want him to be off the chosen path, He doesn't want to have to correct, rebuke, or chasten your husband but God will do it if it has to be done. Be assured, God sees it all and God will correct him. Sometimes, our husbands are doing foolish things and God needs to use us as an Abigail. Abigail has been called a woman of beauty and brains because she made preparations to make up for her husband's foolish actions without telling him. She interceded and humbly went to the man of God, spoke prophetically to him, and saved the lives of her people. Although her husband was acting foolishly, God led her as her husband's help to humbly intervene. We, as wives, must stop at times to consider the weight of the call of a husband. Once he is married that call of a husband is irrevocable because the gift and call of God is irrevocable. Wives, we must consider how difficult it is to meet these standards on a daily basis for someone who is placed in the position of headship, but who is not LORD. God in His position is sovereign, He is Ruler, Creator, and holds all the answers. Your husband, on the other hand, is a human being made in the image of God, given the dominion and authority to lead, but he is still a man – capable of error and prone to mistakes. He is not perfect! He may be in a perfecting state, but he is not perfect – he is not God. We must not expect him to perform or answer as God.

Our headship, our husbands, needs us to remain in

the position to help him. It is vital to understand the part of the body we function in as it relates to being a wife. Remember, we are one body with many members having varying functions. The Lord made man the head of the wife. The wife being closely and directly linked to him can be seen as the neck. I call myself my husband's neck because I understand how these two body parts function simultaneously in unity in the natural. The neck supports the head, the neck holds the head up; the head cannot move or function without the neck. The neck is what connects the head to the rest of the body. The neck is often unnoticed and hardly ever mentioned unless it's broken or not functioning properly; however the neck serves a major role in the body and especially for the head! No one ever says, "WOW! Look at the neck on her!" or "That neck is sexy." Well, although it does not get many compliments and is not recognized for all it does, the neck has an important role to fulfill. The very same is true for you, Woman of God, as a wife, you may go unnoticed by man, you may not receive many compliments, and you may feel over worked and underappreciated, but the fact is that you were created to fulfill a very unique and difficult task – that is – support the head! You never hear from the neck and sometimes as wives are to be a silent vessel that connects the head to the rest of the body – the children, the church, extended family, his purpose, and his destiny. You are the chosen link! Silence in this form does not mean that you, wife, do not have a voice; it is the opposite, you speak loud and clear and are the leader in many forms, you just don't have to use words to accomplish every task. Your actions are your voice – pray for him, intercede for him. You talk to his Head, solicit help from the Father. The change you desire to see will come by prayer because the effectual fervent prayer of the righteous avails much. Prayer changes things.

Many times we are speaking things to the husband trying to get him to change because we witness the behavior and we see the error. If you have a God-fearing husband, don't you know he realizes he is in error? If he is not listening to God, what makes you think he will listen to you! Don't push him away – pray him through! This does not mean you are walking around on mute and that you do not communicate with him at all. Communication is key in any relationship and especially in marriage. What we must master is the art effective communication and how to have healthy conflict. It's after you have the tough conversations and you say those needed helpful things that you leave it in God's hands. I encourage you not to push an issue after you have voiced your concern. It's possible to keep pushing

until you have pushed him right out of the door —
mentally, emotionally, or physically. Or, you can pray
until you have prayed him right into his destiny and
purpose and out of his ignorance. Remember he's
imperfect!

Subject to Him in Everything

Before we end this chapter, we will briefly look at
being subject to him in everything. The ending of
verse 24 says, "Therefore, just as the church is subject
to Christ, so let the wives be to their own husband in
everything." The word "subject" in this verse is the
same Greek work used for the word "submission" in
most of the New Testament scriptures. Therefore,
subjection is actually submission. Submission gets a
bad reputation because, to the carnal eye, it is seen as
being soft or a pushover. The truth is submission is

quiet strength operating to achieve desired prosperous results. One can only obtain the results they desire by submitting and saying, "Not my will, but Thy will be done." Submission takes courage and trust. Submission is not for the faint at heart, submission is not for nonbelievers. This verse instructs wives to be subject to her own husband "in everything." First, let us make sure we understand that when the Bible says "in everything," the Lord means in everything that is not contrary to the will of God. God will not have you subjecting to ungodly and unholy practices and He is definitely not saying submit to a man in abuse. All forms of abuse are contrary to God's word of love. If you are experiencing abuse please seek help and save yourself, especially if it's physical abuse. You are not a punching bag, you are a woman, God's chosen vessel and He will not have you submitting to physical abuse. This is not the time to turn the other cheek. However, Woman of God, you are responsible for submitting to the man of God in everything pertaining to the marriage relationship that is consistent with the laws of God and the Gospel of Christ. Remember you have a responsibility to maintain your very own relationship with the Lord – you must continue to study, have devotion time, prayer time, etc., on your own because you will need the strength from your relationship with God to be the helper to your husband. While your husband is attempting to lead as he feels God is leading him, he needs you to believe in him and support his efforts. Encourage him and allow him to lead. I remember my husband saying to me, "Would you let me lead and stop going around me?" Honestly, I thought I was doing a great job of letting him lead but I found out my way of letting him lead was not his idea of being allowed to lead. I was leaving subtle hints and my body language and facial expressions spoke louder than the actual words. I thought I was doing great by praying for him, but he knew all along that I was not happy and I did not trust his leading because I clearly communicated it with my attitude. Ultimately, I learned that it was not my husband I wasn't trusting, I wasn't trusting God to lead my husband. I wasn't trusting God to speak to him because of what I had seen most often with my natural eye was the man disobeying God and I was angry and frustrated because he was in disobedience which was causing us to suffer. I wanted him to be obedient. I was thinking about our future and our ministry and didn't want him to fail. But I had to trust God; I had to trust that God would and still works all things together for good. I had to trust that God knew how to re-calculate his route if he got off course. I had to trust God. Not trusting God put me in a place of not subjecting or submitting to my husband. I learned that my problem was not with my husband, my problem was with God. I had to repent and get back to the place I was in the beginning. A very wise woman told me, "Do not cease to pray for him and love the man, when you see these things happening, love the man, pray during your quiet time but love the man." Those words stayed with me for several reasons. Once I realized that I had stopped praying for him. I had begun to be very religious, I would pray in the spirit in front of him rebuking the enemy from our home and our marriage, and this infuriated him and made me look stupid because I was not meeting his natural needs. I was not being the natural helper. I called myself rebuking him through praying in the spirit; well all that did was cause more problems. But I heard the woman of God and I did exactly what she said and the turnaround was almost instant. During the beginning of our marriage, I would lay out prostrate before the Lord for my husband four hours a day, five days a week, I was at home while he was at work; so I devoted a portion of my day to praying for him. The results were miraculous! But as we continued in marriage and then the baby came, there was a shift and I stopped praying for him. I began to pray fervently for the baby. Then, God sent the woman of God to remind me to pray for him. I was put here to be his helper and he needed me to help through prayer. I admit I was out of balance, but God! He sent me the help I needed to get back into total alignment with the Word, trusting Him, and being subject to the man. Submit to your imperfect man knowing and trusting that God is the One who is really in control.

CHAPTER 3

RESPECT VS. EXPECTATION

"Nevertheless, let each of you (husband) in particular

so love his own wife as himself and le the wife see

that she respects her husband." Ephesians 5:33

(NKJV)

"Respect your husband" is the phrase I hated hearing in the beginning of our marriage. I could not understand why it appeared that I was always the one getting the instructions on how I should behave in the marriage. I wanted to know when anyone was going to talk to him and hold him accountable for his actions or lack of actions. I was tired of hearing "Chara keep yourself looking nice, buy new clothes, keep your hair together, wear some makeup, complement him, cook, clean, acknowledge him, give him words of affirmation, write him notes, etc." I thought to myself, goodness when is it ever enough? It wasn't until January 2015 that I finally understood why God commanded wives to respect the man. I learned why I kept hearing this list of instructions. First, the list of things for me to do was to be a help for me more than for him. The women of God wanted to make sure I stayed in a good place mentally, emotionally, and spiritually. It was just as important to maintain my sense of individual self and my spiritual relationship with God as it was to maintain my wifely duties. Additionally, they went hand in hand. While I was being built up spiritually, I was putting myself in position of respect and love to the man. In a heated discussion once, I yelled out to my husband, "You do not love me!" and he instantly responded, "You do not respect me!" All along, both of us thought we were loving and respecting one another. The truth is what he was doing to show me love did not speak love to me because it wasn't in the language of love that I speak which is "Acts of Service" (Chapman) and I wasn't speaking respect in the language that speaks love and respect to him which I now know are "Words of Affirmation and Physical Touch" (Chapman). On this day, I asked him, what does disrespect look like to you? He told me when I sit around not taking the time to put myself together and he comes home from work and I look a hot mess (guilty – I'm a stay home mom of a toddler so I didn't feel like I needed to put on good clothes to play in); when he comes in and the home (which is school also) is not together; when I am too busy working on ministry, books, businesses, etc. and I don't make it my business to show affection by giving him hugs or holding his hands and when I show lack of appreciation by not acknowledging how hard he works and when I don't say I'm proud of him. WOW! I was blown aback. But I was guilty as charged with my saved, sanctified, spirit-filled self! I have the most affectionate husband ever and I was too busy being caught up in the day to day demands of "life" and I was not caught up in the day to day duties and joy of "marriage."

I began the marriage with excellence in the area of respect. But at some point, I stopped respecting him and I started expecting from him. I expected him to love me, work, bring in the money, take the baby out to play after he came home so I could have a break, help me with meals, give me time to write, take me out, have fun with me, pray with us, minister to us, do bible study with us, talk to me...and the list goes on. I was putting all these demands on this imperfect man without reciprocating anything in return that he considered respect or love. I learned that having these great expectations in this man put him in position to fail and that put even more pressure on him. The bible does not tell us to expect from man, it tells us to respect the husband. We are to have our expectations in the Lord and Him only. We are to respect his hard work, respect his leadership efforts, respect his love and affection, respect his loyalty, respect his faithfulness; we are to respect what he brings to the table. Then we are to expect God to bring him (the husband) to the place in God of perfection (maturity), fullness, and completeness. How do we respect the things he is doing? Tell him, show affection and appreciation, take care of ourselves, put his needs before ours, speak life to him, and allow him to make a mistake without pestering him about it, while being there when he does fall to offer hugs, love, and affection - letting him know he is not a failure and assure him that he will succeed and he will not let us fail. To the man, respect is love; therefore, love him by respecting him. Putting expectations on him will weaken his spirit. This is the reason we see many husbands walking around with false smiles and you can see the division in the marriage. He is attempting to live up to the expectations of his wife and God. Free him from your expectations so he can walk in the will of God and meet God's expectation of him as a husband, leader, and child of God.

When we hold our husbands in expectation, the ultimate result is disrespect. Far too many marriages are ending because of the level of disrespect the men experience. Wives, you may display a strong level of disrespect to the gifts, the calling, and the anointing on his life if you perceive he is not representing Christ in totality. When the man of God is preaching and ministering, while tearing up the house of God, and his behavior and character does not match outside of the church (or whatever job he is working) it becomes difficult for you to overlook it. It's difficult to be his "number one cheerleader" because you are in disbelief of the two different personalities you witness exuding from him. Your heart's desire is that your husband will heed the voice of God, obey His commands, lead according to God's plan and purpose, and walk as a man with integrity - being a doer of the Word - and not just a man who reads and preaches it. You desire this whether he is a preacher, a principal, a gardener, or an entrepreneur, you desire him to accomplish it "as unto the Lord." You find it difficult to respect and receive from him when he is "performing" and not meeting his potential and you are hurting to your core because you see destiny in the man. The truth is you have become angry with him for what he is doing to God! Disrespect has manifested because you are walking in unforgiveness. You have not forgiven him for disobeying God, you have not forgiven him for not leading according to the Word, you have not forgiven him for his lack of study and prayer in your home, you have not forgiven him for his lack of interest in his own spiritual growth and development as you see him ministering to everyone else but not taking care of the evil and demonic forces in his own life; and you have not forgiven him for not living a life of holiness before the children. You desire to see the same pulpit man in your home when in reality what you get at home is definitely the carnal man and you are upset! This happens if you married the man because you were attracted to the anointing or if you married him because he is the God-ordained man for your life. The truth is you see the best in your husband and hate to see him not living up to his God-given potential. It infuriates you to see him disrespecting and dishonoring God. You want to know how he can demand so much from others when he is not giving the same effort. How can he speak on something he is not doing himself? Trust me woman of God, I get it, I understand! But you must forgive him. You must forgive him for how he has treated God. You have his best interest at heart and you love God with all your heart, mind, and soul; but unforgiveness toward him will not change the situation; unforgiveness will lead to hatred and divorce, which are not a part of God's plan for your marriage. Forgive him and free yourself! Allow God to change his heart because your unforgiveness and disgruntled attitude will not change his heart. His heart is in God's hand and God is in control. Earlier we discussed how you are to submit to him in everything – everything that is in line with God's commands and the Gospel of Christ. Therefore, respect his behavior and the areas of sin you see manifesting. Yes, respect them, but it doesn't mean you are obligated to participate in the areas of sin. Make sure you continue obeying the Lord – please understand that the Lord is not going to have you do anything that will usurp your husband's authority, but He will give you wisdom on how to function in your marriage until your husband's behavior is in total alignment with God's will and plan for his life. Continue to pray for him and do as I was instructed you to do – love the man. You can do this, trust me, you do it all the time when you respect people's lifestyle that are living as fornicators, homosexuals, drug abusers, liars, thieves, gossips, etc. You respect what they do and you continue to love them but you do not participate in the actions or behaviors, yet you pray for them and continue to love them and minister to them in love. Well the same will be true in this case, respect his behavior, love him, pray for him, and be the help you were created to be, "the neck" behind the scenes interceding on his behalf. God is not mad at him and you should not be mad either. Free him by forgiving him. Once you forgive him, you will be free to love him. Your expression of love and respect is directly linked to your forgiveness. Don't expect him to live to your standards, respect his efforts and pray for change.

Further, I encourage you to learn your husbands love language so you can love him in the language he understands. If you are touching him all the time and touch is not his love language then you are speaking Spanish to an English speaking man which is the reason he is unresponsive to your efforts. There are many marriage books to help you along this journey, invest in some other books to become the wife who respects her husband. Finally, on this topic, stop being so spiritual, you were created a spiritual being in a natural body that requires natural nourishment to survive. As a wife, part of your natural nourishment is love and affection. There are way too many benefits to enjoy in marriage to be stuck in the pits of destruction because you won't submit and respect this man. Respect him and begin to enjoy the perks and benefits of marriage; after all, the perks were designed for you to enjoy in the union of the marriage institution. You have a legal right to enjoy. Break the disrespect barrier that is hindering your marriage from pure godly pleasure! Free him from your expectations so you can be free to enjoy your marriage, because you are missing out on all the wonderful benefits of being married. Woman of God, free him – he is imperfect!

CHAPTER 4

HIS IMPERFECTION

"Wives, likewise, be submissive to our own husbands, that even if some do not obey the word, they without a word, may be won by the conduct of their wives, when they observe your chaste conduct accompanied by fear." (1 Peter 3:1-2)

In the previous chapter, we discussed respecting him even if he is not doing what we know he should do as a man, a man of God. In 1 Peter 3:1-2, the writer confirms that our quiet godly behavior (conduct) and upright attitude will draw the man to Christ and help him get to the place of obedience. Therefore, I urge you to look at submission as a privilege, a strategy, and a tool to help dig your husband out of the pit.

Look at submission as an opportunity for ministry. Jesus gave us the model of submission when He was on the cross.

When Jesus was on the cross fulfilling His destiny, His hands were nailed in a position that would not allow Him to touch anyone else, heal anyone else, or help anyone else, even if He wanted to. His feet were nailed to the cross and He could not go another step further to do any more work. At this point, His work was on the cross! In this position, our Savior only had access to use His words and what He did in His model of submission on the cross was pray and make declarations for His bride. He prayed for forgiveness stating that "they know not what they do," He prayed for His immediate family a prayer of comfort and assurance. He made declarations of "I thirst" and "It is finished," as He yielded to completing the work of submitting His life to the

Father for the sins of the world. He submitted for justification, He submitted for sanctification, He submitted to take the pressure off of us! His submission set us free and guaranteed us a chance at eternal life in heaven. His submission gave us the ultimate victory. His submission saved our lives! Wife, you too have this unique position of submission! I implore you to wear it as a badge of honor. Humble yourself, submit to your man of God, submit to the call of living a quiet life of prayer and intercession with godly conduct that will ultimately win your husband. Live according to God's word and allow God to use your life the way He used the life of Jesus! When you want to put your hands in it, remember you are on the cross. When you want to walk and fix things yourself, remember you are on the cross. You move as God leads you to move, but if He has you standing still with your feet nailed - stay on the cross, and don't come down until He releases you to do so. People are watching your marriage and watching how you will handle situations. It is imperative for you to remain in one position. Continue practicing the spiritual disciplines of fasting and praying, celebration and joy, praise and worship, and times of solitude. These practices will keep your mind stayed on Jesus and will keep you in perfect peace while God is doing a work in the man through your behavior. A few years ago, my husband was asked, "How did you get so serious about your walk with the Lord man, because it seems like when you went in you went all in?" His response was, "I watched my wife! I watched how she prayed about everything; I saw how she spoke the word for EVERYTHING. I witnessed her fast and saw the results. I watched her tithe and saw the results. My wife is the reason I am where I am today in God." I take no credit for anything that he said, but I blessed

God for using me as a vessel to draw the man nigh unto Him. All I did was live my life the way I was accustomed to living it and that is according to the Word of God. You may have noticed that when I met my husband he was not living according to the bible. Actually, he wasn't even saved. I remember when he gave his life to the Lord – it was 2 months after we got married. When we met, I never moved away from my faith or my moral values. He wanted to have dates on the days I was attending church and that meant that he would need to attend with me and he did. I refused to compromise to something that would lead me astray. I respected his plans for wanting to take me out but I made sure those plans would not interfere with my biblical standards. Little did I know God was using me to draw my husband to Him, it had nothing to do with me - I was only the vessel. I was a submitted vessel to the Lord and upon marriage I became a submitted vessel to my own husband. Submission relinquishes control and opens up avenues of trust; to submit to your own husband is an act of respect in his eyes. If you are bound by a controlling spirit, then submission will be a major area that God wants to purify in your life. What better way to walk out your deliverance from control than by relinquishing control in your marriage, submitting to your husband (as to the Lord).

According to scripture, we notice the writer telling the wives to love their "own husband." This tells me that wives may have the tendency to demonstrate love, respect, honor, and appreciation to others outside of the chosen man of God for our lives. This does not necessarily mean the wife is in the act of physical adultery, but there is spiritual adultery and emotional adultery. There are times when wives put their pastor or spiritual leader's needs before the needs of her own husband and this is error. Yes, it is appropriate to honor the set vessel of the house of God, but that vessel is just set over the house of God, not over your home. It is an error to leave your husband unattended while participating in absolutely everything the church is hosting and sponsoring. Your first ministry is your husband. There is no reason to bounce around fixing pastors plate, getting him water, taking him towels, etc., there is probably a chosen vessel to handle these tasks. Focus on cooking and fixing plates for your own husband because just as sure as you are attempting to take care of the husband that is not yours, there is a woman watching and waiting her turn to take care of yours. It may be easy to fall into this practice because the vessel of the house has been delivering words that have helped you and that is understandable, but remember he is doing his job. It's his duty to deliver those words, he's not doing it to flatter you (I hope). He's doing it to help you, to feed your spirit, help you grow and mature; he's doing his job of shepherding the sheep. That's all you are - sheep! Get spiritually fed, then go home and submit to your own husband!

Additionally, this verse clearly states that "some (men) do not obey the Word." This is implying he is imperfect. The word perfect in the Greek means "maturity," as it does in Hebrews 6:1. When we talk about loving the man in his imperfection, we love him in his immaturity. We love him in his immaturity simply because he will never be perfect in the sense of being blameless or without error. If he could be without error then he would not have needed a helper in the first place. Understand that everyone matures differently – at different times, in different circumstances, etc. That means it is unproductive to compare where your husband is mentally, emotionally, spiritually, or financially with another man. He may not have had the appropriate training; he may be un-teachable in his immaturity; he may be a slow learner; or he may be bound by fear. Whatever is holding up his progression needs to be addressed in prayer, not in comparison or negative remarks. Remember the Lord already knows he is prone to error, imperfect, and immature and he created you to win him by your conduct. It's the Word, not my opinion! You can help him mature, you have to love him and love him wholeheartedly while he walks through immaturity, love him while he progresses from milk to meat. What's interesting is that the Lord did not wait for him to mature or become perfect before joining you as one. He joined you as one then instructed you to help him mature! You can do this – submit (relinquish control) to your own husband, that if he does not obey the Word (is imperfect/immature) you will win him (help him) by your behavior (holiness, spiritual disciplines, gentle and quiet spirit in the correct position) when he observes (sees) your chaste conduct accompanied by fear (reverence of the Lord).

CHAPTER 5

LOVING THE MAN

One of the most daunting tasks to complete is loving someone who constantly hurts you! It hurts when his words come at you like a dagger. It's hurtful when promises are broken. It hurts when everyone and everything is made a priority over you and you are left waiting for your opportunity to experience joyful times with him. It hurts when women and men are allowed to disrespect you. It hurts when he has become emotionally, spiritually, or physically connected with someone else. It hurts when you are loving him and he is not reciprocating the same love, yet you continue to love him. Then you even turn your love up a notch. You begin to go outside of your comfort zone to prove love to him and your efforts go unnoticed and unwanted. It hurts when home is not financially taken care of yet his material possessions continue to increase in number. It hurts when you get a medical diagnosis that requires you to change your lifestyle and he won't help or participate in it with you. It hurts when what you love is not important to him. It hurts you to love when what you really want to do is leave.

You may be suffering from years of afflicted mishaps that have caused your heart to harden towards him. Woman of God, it may hurt but you are commanded to love him through it all! No, you are not commanded to be a fool, but you are now one flesh and you vowed to love him through thick and thin, for better or for worse, through sickness and health until death separates you. God can create in you a clean heart; one free from hurt, anger, bitterness, and resentment. God can renew a steadfast spirit within you. God can show you how to extend extra grace toward the husband that is hurting you. It is not His will for you to live a life of hurt, however, hurt does creep in and when it arises it's designed to divide you and tear you apart. You must know that the enemy hates unity and agreement which is why when the two become one, he (the enemy) magnifies small things to make them appear big or out of order. You have to know why you were put with this man, you must know your husband's heart and not see his flesh. Always remember that the enemy will use anyone who is open and available. He used Eve to deceive Adam and separate them and that viscous cycle continues today.

There was a time at the beginning of my marriage when I thought I was going to lose my mind. I thought why did God put me with this man and why is He allowing me to go through all of this! Honestly, it was one thing after another, and I grew very feeble in my spirit. Whenever I went to church and there was a "word" for me from the Lord, it was the same message, "Daughter, don't be weary in well doing." Honestly, I was frustrated and terribly confused – why do I keep getting this word to not be weary and why isn't anyone correcting him from wearying me?! Then, God began to show me my husband's heart. I had to live with the knowledge of his potential, not with is manifested actions. I was required to love him regardless of how the enemy was using him. After so much hurt, it was difficult to even lie next to him in the bed because I felt like I was sleeping with the enemy. Honestly, I didn't want those things to transfer to me – it was an inward and an outward battle. I spent days praying in my home, anointing his clothes and shoes, declaring that his steps are ordered by the Lord. I learned how to love him how God loves us, while we were hurting Him.

In the 3rd year of our marriage, another woman became our issue. I remember this day all too well. I was home praying on his behalf and as I was ending the prayer I had a vision of a tall light brown woman with long auburn colored hair, she was wearing a red dress and had her hands on her wide curvy hips, smoking a cigarette, while smiling a devilish smile. It was eerie but I knew it was a vision from the Lord. My husband followed a predictable routine daily (and he still does), I knew the times to expect his call and everyday like clockwork he called; well that is every day except the day I had the vision of the woman (we will call her Missy). When he did call me, the conversation was different and his tone was distant. What normally is a 15 minute conversation was a 30 second conversation. I asked, "Are you okay?" He said, "Yea, I'm good." If you knew my husband you would know that is not how he speaks. I didn't force anything I just said, "Okay, see you later, love you." He barely responded, "Love you too." Upon his arrival home, I asked how his day went and he proceeded to tell me a new crew of people started work. Then, I asked did that group include a woman and I described what she looked like and my husband's eyes nearly popped out of his head. He asked how I knew. I explained that the Lord showed me and I went on to explain that she was on an assignment from the pit of hell to destroy marriage - our marriage. She looked like the type of woman he would have chosen versus me, remember I stated earlier we were not one another's ideal choice.

As time went on, the Lord would show me her plans and what she was doing. Our youth ministry had a fundraiser with candy bars, she bought every candy bar he had in the boxes. She learned that he was a minister and she began to "seek counsel" telling him all about her sad life story. She acknowledged all that I was doing for him and she complimented him on how wonderful his wife is to prepare him such great meals every day. What he was not seeing is how subtly she was moving in. When she talked to him about what I fixed for breakfast, she asked him if he had a favorite cereal and he told her what they were. She went out and bought his favorite cereal so he would have a backup in the event I didn't send him with food. My husband is brutally honest so he told me everything that was happening. As she poured out her life story she pretended to hang onto his every word of advice and "counsel." And every day she needed new advice. The entire time this is happening, I'm home praying and interceding and the Lord was showing me her next move. I continued to warn my husband who began showing great disinterest in me. I noticed he began to touch me less, when he went to bed he stopped cuddling with me like he did every night, he began to sleep with his back turned to me with a huge space between us, and his conversation with me was almost nonexistent. He called me from work like normal but there was nothing to talk about. I was losing him. However, I was praying diligently and the Lord was giving me strategy. He instructed me to amp up my love, show extra grace, go the extra mile – He instructed me to fight. I was warring in the spirit pulling down strongholds but loving in the natural. This proved to be the most difficult task ever because what I wanted to do was get in the car and go out there and kick her tail. But God has an awesome way of maturing you and sharpening your spiritual gifts. It was during this time in our marriage that we only had one vehicle and my driver's license was suspended so I couldn't drive if I wanted to. I was trapped in a position of learning strategic warfare. That is what I did – I went to war. Laying on my face one day, the Lord showed me that Missy was going to try to get into our home. We had begun to overcome this barrier because he began to see her ways and he started listening to God. The Lord began to speak to his heart. We started our preparation of getting the nursery ready for the child we were believing God for, and that meant we needed to sale some furniture. One piece we were looking to sale was our beautiful gold chaise lounge. On the day I had the vision of her trying to come into our home, as I was getting up from laying on my face, my husband called me, it was his morning break. After I said hello, I immediately said, "Missy is going to try to come into our home, be careful." There was an awkward silence. I said, "Hello, Honey are you there?" With a broken tone and embarrassment in his voice, he said, "She just offered to buy the chaise lounge at whatever price we want to sell it for." I said,

"Oh! How is she going to get it because she is not coming here, and you are not delivering it to her!" Then the man of God said, "No! We will sell it to somebody else, she is not getting into our home." Several more weeks passed and he finally sat her down and told her that whatever was happening had to stop, he told her he was at work and could not minister to her anymore, if she needed some counsel she would need to make an appointment to meet with both of us. He told her they had gotten too close and too personal and he told her "it ends today." Missy broke down crying. My husband ended their "relationship," she had fallen in "lust" with him and he was committing spiritual and emotional adultery. He called me to tell me what happened and he was in total disbelief and shock. He said, "I didn't know she thought we were in a relationship, she knew I am married." It was a long and rough few months but I fought like a soldier. I prayed and went to war on the enemy for my marriage, nevertheless I was hurt. When he told me what happened that morning I broke down in tears – my husband was committing adultery and it was the worst kind of adultery to me – she had his attention! I craved his attention but she had it. I cried profusely and I hurt to my core. He called me several times that day and he eventually left work early to come home to see about me – he knew I was hurt. He apologized to me and repented. He did explain to me that it became easy to talk to her and that she made him feel important and smart because she wanted to hear what he had to say. I knew what she was issuing out was false, but in his imperfection she was meeting a need that I did not meet. I was focused on being a wife and stopped being a friend. I was focused on us doing ministry and not allowing him to minister to me. I was focused on taking care of the home while she was taking care of him mentally. Yes, I was doing wife duties, but it was not what he felt that he needed. In his imperfection he was desiring his fleshly desires to be met and I was not meeting those. I was meeting natural and spiritual desires, but what he craved I did not provide. The enemy knows that my husband will not physically commit adultery because of his honor and value of marriage. Therefore, the enemy appealed to the neglected un-renewed area of his mind and sent someone to meet his un-renewed carnal desires to feel like "the man," he wanted to feel important. He wanted somebody to listen to him and to acknowledge his words. He wanted a cheerleader and I did not know how to be a cheerleader because I couldn't cheer for what I disagreed with. My unwillingness to compromise and stroke his ego almost cost me my marriage. Even though God was attempting to heal him in areas and deliver him from people pleasing, I was not helping in his deliverance by being too spiritual and being too independent. Being a homemaker comes with disadvantages that can hurt a marriage if it's not balanced. Being home doing all the home duties put me in position where I didn't need to ask for help often, I did it myself and he felt unneeded. I was great with prayer so I did not go to him often to pray for me and he felt unneeded. I had a ministry that was growing rapidly, and he felt unneeded because there wasn't much for him to do. I was doing great as far as I knew, but I was doing terrible at helping the king in him rise up. I knew he was a leader and had great potential but I wasn't a needy person and he needed to be needed. I had to learn to need him. I began needing him in small things to teach me how to need him and depend on him. I started needing help with opening jars, carrying groceries, etc. Although it seemed petty to me, the Lord was teaching me how to be interdependent. Eventually, I began noticing that I really did need him and it wasn't difficult to seek the help. As time continued on, I found myself actually needing him for hugs and conversation. God had broken down a wall in me that I had built to protect me from being hurt. I had built a wall of independence. We can't be so independent that we don't need help, because it will linger on in our marriage causing a communication barrier. Communication barriers are the beginning of infidelity.

God had to heal my heart and mend our marriage. That night when he tried to commune with me, my body would not respond and I knew we were in for a long recovery. My body rejected him because I was suffering from the hurt of infidelity. The both of us began to pray and ask God to intervene. We went to marriage counseling and God began to heal each of us – and our marriage. I learned a lot from this experience of hurt and infidelity. I learned how to tap into a spiritual realm that would show me the plans of the enemy; I learned how to do strategic warfare. I learned how to love my husband when I knew he was not loving me. I learned how to intercede for more than my marriage; I interceded for his life, his anointing, his call, and his destiny. I interceded for his spiritual eyes to be opened. I learned to pray and put a demand on a manifestation. I learned how to trust God to move in his life. I also learned that my imperfect husband was in need of natural affection as well as spiritual affection. I learned that I did not want to lose my husband although he was imperfect. It taught me not to focus on his imperfection but to see him as a perfecting man of God who is walking out his deliverance, attempting to please God and please me.

Ultimately, what my perfecting husband needed had to come from God, but I was not helping by brushing him off when he needed me the most. I had to humble myself, seek God's face, and allow Him to heal the land – He healed our marriage.

This woman "Missy" finally conquered another married man on that job and I was still crushed because I hate the plan of the enemy. Once I learned she was actually sleeping with a married man of God I continued to pray strategically until she was removed from the place of business. Sometimes we will need to pray for other marriages when we see the enemy attempting to destroy what God has joined together. In all this, my husband received deliverance and growth in the area of seeking the approval of people and that made the fight worth it. Wives, we are joined with the man of God to help him in his imperfection. Again, marriage is not meant to make you happy, it's meant to make you holy!

This particular situation with my husband caused me to understand that I am commanded to love even in the midst of dysfunction and chaos. Ask Hosea! God called Hosea to marry an impure woman, love her fully, and have children with her; then go after her and bring her back when she strays. (Hosea 3:1) Hosea's calling was to show, by his own love for Gomer, the kind of love God has for the land of Israel. Hosea knew he was marrying an immoral woman but Hosea was learning what God goes through when He constantly loves us after we stray, disobey Him, and dishonor Him. Hosea's marriage is a template of how we are to love our husband, even in dysfunction – in his imperfection. God knew who He was joining together and He knew the baggage coming along with each person, yet He called you to that specific mate for His specific purpose. Once your mind can comprehend that your marriage is not about you, then it will be easier for you to love him.

CONCLUSION

Before we can completely understand how to love a person here on earth, we must understand we are only able to love because God first loved us. If He had not loved us, we would not have the capability to love, we would not have a model to reflect; but He (God) gave us an example to follow – and that example is found in God. Before we can love another person, we must first wholeheartedly seek, hunger, and thirst to know and understand the encompassing greatness of the love God has for us – His created beings. God loves us in our perfecting state. He loves us in every mistake, every sin, every evil thought. He loves us! He requires us to grow and to mature, but in order to grow and to mature we must experience some hard falls, learn some hard lessons, and walk out some deliverance. With your husband as your God barometer, you will learn how much more pruning and molding you need.

Maturity does not happen overnight; therefore, do not expect your husband to get it all right overnight – or ever. Remember, he is an imperfect man going through a perfecting process. There may be generational barriers that need to be broken, there may be ungodly soul ties that need to be broken, or there may be some cultural barriers that need to be broken, whatever state he is in when you marry him, just know God will use the marriage to help both of you mature in God. Maturing in Him causes a manifestation of maturing in moral character and integrity. He will never be blameless and without sin, but love him. Love him in is imperfection – love him to his mature state, love him to his purpose and destiny.

"For this reason I bow my knees to the Father of our Lord Jesus Christ, from whom the whole family in heaven and earth is named, that He would grant you according to the riches of His glory, to be strengthened with might through His Spirit in the inner man, that Christ may dwell in your hearts through faith; that you, being rooted and grounded in love, may be able to comprehend with all the saints what is the width and length and depth and height – to know the love of Christ which passes knowledge; that you may be filled with the fullness of God" (Ephesians 3:14-19 NKJV)

The love you have for the man in his imperfection is a love that passes knowledge. Let go of what you think you know about love and love him the way God instructs you to; love him how God loves you, unconditionally.

NOTES

1. New Spirit Filled Life Bible (NKJV)

2. "Strong's Exhaustive Concordance" James Strong

3. www.merriam-dictionary.com (web)

4. "Five Love Languages" Gary Chapman

ABOUT THE AUTHOR

Pastor and Overseer Chara A. Taylor is a River of Joy. She began her ministry for the Lord in February 2006, as she launched out in the deep with the mentoring ministry of GEWWELS Inc. (Girls Entering Womanhood While Experiencing Life's Struggles), a ministry encouraging young women to trust God and pursue holiness as they journey through life's struggles transitioning from adolescence to womanhood as the Bible tells us to be holy in all manner of conduct (1 Peter 1:15). It's a ministry of self-awareness and holiness to girls ages 12 - 21. Her mission is to inspire females to understand their individual purpose in Christ, propelling them to shine in that purpose, not being overcome by evil but by overcoming life's obstacles while still living holy.

Pastor Chara truly believes that we are fearfully and wonderfully made to do the will of the Father uniquely as He created us all differently - therefore she encourages young people to learn their gifts and operate / SHINE in that gift/gifts. Her motto scripture is Romans 8:28 "for all things work together for good to those who love God and are the called according to His purpose." Pastor Chara receives great joy from seeing people and businesses go forth in what God has purposed for them.

Pastor Chara carries a smile that brightens up the room and heals people in their desolate places. She is outgoing, bold, and not afraid to go to war with the enemy. Pastor Chara is an effective teacher, preacher, and intercessor for Jesus Christ. She has served as Master of Ceremony for several events and services. She has ministered at 100 Women in White services. She has led various workshops to young women. She hosts an annual Shine in Purpose Conference for young women in St. Louis MO and an annual Mother Daughter Banquet for mothers and daughters to connect and reconnect. She received a Bachelors of Science degree in Christian Ministry in May 2014 from St. Louis Christian College, where she graduated top of the class as Valedictorian and was inducted in the Honor Societies of The Association of Biblical Higher Learning, Stone-Campbell Journal Honors, and Sigma Lambda Chi-Chi, with the help of God.

In July 2014, Chara was elevated to Overseer by her spiritual parents and covering Apostles Robbie and Sharon Peters of Kingdom Empowerment International Covenant of Fellowship Churches, Inc. She loves family and having fun!

One of her greatest testimonies is the miracle birth of Isaac Jeremiah Taylor, her baby boy! After being told she would not conceive - God miraculously gave her the child she longed and prayed for 5 years. In this, she learned how to keep the faith in God, continue to do His work, trust His timing...She learned that waiting on Lord does pay off. She has launched Hannah's Cry prayer call to inspire other married women and couples who are waiting and believing God for a child. She launched Bible Babies Inc., a retail store of biblically inspired clothing for babies. Further, along with her husband Bishop-Designate Ronald, she assists inspiring couples to live godly marriages according to Ephesians 5. Their One-Flesh Ministry is called Ephesians 5 Husbands and

Wives. Overseer aspires to do things Gods' way, which is why she believes in living Holy, in fear and reverence of the Lord always. Overseer believes if you live biblical principles, you will receive biblical promises!